# Reducing Your Carbon Footprint in the Kitchen

Linley Erin Hall

New York

Published in 2009 by The Rosen Publishing Group, Inc.
29 East 21st Street, New York, NY 10010



First Edition



**Library of Congress Cataloging-in-Publication Data**

Hall, Linley Erin.
Reducing your carbon footprint in the kitchen / Linley Erin Hall.
p. cm.—(Your carbon footprint)
Includes bibliographical references and index.
ISBN-13: 978-1-4042-1776-8 (lib. bdg.)
1. Green movement. 2. Environmental responsibility. 3. Organic living. 4. Sustainable living. 5. Recycling (Waste, etc.) 6. Carbon dioxide. I. Title.
GE195.H345 2008
641.5—dc22

2008005614

*Manufactured in the United States of America*

**On the cover:** Top left: Farmers' markets are an excellent source of fresh fruits and vegetables. Bottom left: Reusable rather than disposable containers can be used to store a wide variety of foods. Right: Energy-efficient appliances can help reduce a family's carbon footprint.

# Contents


| | | |
|---|---|---|
| | Introduction | 4 |
| 1 | Eating More Sustainably | 6 |
| 2 | At the Grocery Store | 16 |
| 3 | While Cooking | 24 |
| 4 | Beyond the Kitchen | 31 |
| | Glossary | 38 |
| | For More Information | 40 |
| | For Further Reading | 42 |
| | Bibliography | 43 |
| | Index | 46 |

# Introduction

Everything that humans do has an impact on the environment. A carbon footprint is a way to measure the impact of some of those human activities. The "carbon" in "carbon footprint" refers to carbon dioxide. This gas is essential to plant growth. However, carbon dioxide is also the most common greenhouse gas. These gases are building up in Earth's atmosphere, resulting in global warming and climate change.

Greenhouse gases absorb sunlight in the atmosphere. This makes the air surrounding Earth warmer. Global warming is an increase in the average temperature of Earth's atmosphere. This causes changes in climate on Earth's surface. Although the atmosphere is getting warmer, Earth's surface isn't warming everywhere. The process of global warming may actually make some places colder. For this reason, many people talk about climate change rather than global warming.

The primary source of carbon dioxide in the atmosphere is the burning of fossil fuels. Fossil fuels include oil, coal, and natural gas. These fuels were created from living things through processes that took millions of years. Humans get much of the energy they use from the burning of fossil fuels to create electricity. Fossil fuels also power vehicles in the form of gasoline. Thus, to reduce their carbon footprints, people need to use less energy overall. Much of the energy they do use should come from sources that are not fossil fuels, such as the wind and sun.

To live more sustainably, or to "live green," means to take actions and choose products that will reduce a person's impact on the environment. People around the world are making changes in their lives to reduce their carbon footprints. Companies are also improving how they make products in order to be more environmentally friendly. Some changes are big; others are small. All make a difference.

The burning of fossil fuels produces most of the electricity used in the United States. However, doing so also damages the environment.

People can make changes in all aspects of their lives, but right at home is a good place to start. The jet fuel that airplanes use produces a lot of carbon dioxide. But most people don't fly on planes every day. Everyone needs to eat every day, however. As a result, changing what and how we eat can make a large impact on our carbon footprints. For this reason, the kitchen is a good place to begin creating a more environmentally friendly lifestyle. The following chapters will present some things that kids and their families can do to reduce the amount of energy that goes into preparing the food they eat.

# 1 Eating More Sustainably

Something is sustainable when it has the ability to continue being used—and reused—while having a minimal effect on the environment. For example, cutting down, or clear-cutting, all the trees in a forest is not sustainable. Eventually, the forest is gone. The trees might grow back again, but it could take hundreds of years for the forest to be like it once was. Harvesting a forest's older trees while carefully tending and nurturing its younger growth and planting new trees is a more sustainable way to obtain wood for fuel, paper, and building materials.

Similarly, using lots of fossil fuels to provide energy for human activities is not sustainable. Supplies of fossil fuels are limited. Because humans have already taken so much oil from the planet, it's getting harder to extract what is left. In addition, burning fossil fuels produces greenhouse gases that are causing Earth's climate to change. If unchecked, this climate change could have huge effects on life on Earth. Ecosystems are already changing in noticeable ways. This is why it's so important for everyone to reduce their carbon footprints wherever possible.

When deciding on products to buy or actions to take, it's important to look at how much energy the product or action uses. And lots of energy goes into the food we eat.

These seedlings will eventually become trees to replace those logged in this forest. However, trees take years to grow. To ensure supplies of wood, paper, and other products, forests need to be logged sustainably.

## Energy and Food

Food production requires energy. Even before a person turns on the microwave to heat a TV dinner, a lot of energy has gone into that food.

First, a farmer grew and harvested the raw materials. Crops need water. This often must be pumped to the fields, which takes energy. Many farming techniques also require the use of chemical fertilizer, a substance that is used to add nutrients to soil. Farmers may also use

A farm worker adjusts sprinkler heads spraying water on a field. Such irrigation systems use energy that is part of the carbon footprint of the food that is grown. Pesticides, herbicides, farm machinery, and transportation of harvested crops also contribute to a food's carbon footprint.

pesticides or herbicides to help keep insects and weeds away. These chemicals may be made from fossil fuels, and energy was used to make them in any case. Some crops are harvested using machines, which require fuel to run. Raising animals also requires energy: to transport water and animal feed to the farm, to light and heat the buildings, and even to slaughter the animals.

After harvesting the raw materials, machines cooked and packaged the food at a processing plant. Energy is used to transport the raw materials to the plant. Preparing a food usually involves heating it. Energy is needed to create heat. The machines at the plant also need energy to keep running, and energy was used to create the packaging, or container, that the food ends up in.

After processing, trucks transported the frozen dinner to the supermarket. These likely used fossil fuels as energy. Freezers in the truck, the supermarket, and at home kept the frozen dinner cold until it went in the microwave. The freezers and microwave all need energy to keep working.

Most of the energy in this process came from fossil fuels. Thus, food production can significantly contribute to climate change. But there are many ways to reduce one's carbon footprint in this process of getting food from farm to your plate.

## Food Miles

The concept of food miles refers to the distance that a unit of food traveled between the farm where it was grown or raised and your dinner table. One of the biggest sources of carbon dioxide in the air is burning gasoline in cars, trucks, airplanes, and other vehicles. Reducing the number of miles that food travels lowers its environmental impact.

For example, when it is winter in the Northern Hemisphere, some grocery stores sell produce that was grown in the Southern Hemisphere or nearer the equator, where temperatures are warmer. While strawberries from Chile or Mexico may offer a taste of summer when three feet of snow are piled up outside, this fruit has traveled hundreds or thousands of miles, requiring transport by plane, boat, train, and/or truck to reach

The gasoline that fuels automobiles is made from oil, a fossil fuel. Transporting food from one place to another thus uses energy. One way to reduce your carbon footprint is to buy foods that have traveled only short distances instead of around the world.

the supermarket. All that traveling uses a lot of fossil fuel energy, not only to fuel the vehicles but also to keep the fruit cold so that it is still fresh when it reaches the store.

In contrast, fruits and vegetables that come from a nearby farm might have traveled only twenty-five miles (forty kilometers) to reach the supermarket. To really reduce food miles, people can grow their own vegetables and fruits in a backyard garden or in indoor pots. You can preserve, can, or freeze your own fruit and vegetables for use in winter and spring, when fresh local produce is not available. Some grocery stores also sell local canned and frozen foods.

## Processing and Packaging

Foods that are highly processed have used more energy by the time they reach the grocery store than have ones that are less processed. Processing is anything that changes the food from the form it is in right after harvesting. This can include making smaller pieces (by grinding wheat into flour or dicing fruit, for example), cooking, or mixing with other foods.

After being picked, an apple requires only the energy it takes to get from farm to market. When an apple goes into a jar of applesauce before reaching the market, however, much more energy is necessary. This energy includes the fuel to transport the apples to a factory and electricity to run the machines that cook the apples, puree them, and squirt the sauce into jars. Creating the jars that hold the applesauce also requires energy. And, of course, the jars must eventually be transported to the supermarket. Therefore, a family can reduce its carbon footprint by eating less processed foods whenever possible. If you have a choice between an apple and applesauce, choose the apple.

Processed foods are likely to have more packaging, whether it be boxes, bags, jars, bottles, cans, or other containers, than do less processed foods. Energy is required to make these packages. First, people must extract the raw material. This can include drilling oil (for plastics), chopping down trees (for paper and cardboard), or mining for metals (for aluminum and tin containers). Then the raw materials must

An orchard brims with ripe Elstar apples. One way to reduce your carbon footprint is to eat fresh apples and other fruits instead of buying processed versions, such as applesauce. More energy is needed to cook and package applesauce than simply to transport apples from the same orchard to the supermarket.

be transformed into packaging, which may involve melting, shaping, chemical reactions, and other processes. Foods must then be placed in the packages and the packages sealed, and energy is needed to run the equipment that performs these operations.

Buying foods that have less packaging can help reduce a family's carbon footprint. Some stores now sell goods like cereals, nuts, pasta, grains, coffee, and dried fruits in bulk bins, allowing you to fill your own reusable container with them, thereby avoiding cardboard boxes (which require the destruction of trees) and plastic containers (which take a lot of energy and pollution to produce and take thousands of years to decompose in landfills after they are used).

## Organic vs. Conventional

Conventional farming techniques often use pesticides, herbicides, chemical fertilizers, and other substances to help crops grow. Organic foods are those that were grown or raised without using most such chemicals. For example, organic farms may rely on insects to eat other bugs that eat crops. Organic farmers also use compost—a mixture of decaying organic matter, such as food scraps and dead leaves—to fertilize their crops.

According to the scientific journal *Nature*, a growing body of research suggests that organic farming is more environmentally friendly than conventional, pesticide- and fertilizer-based farming. In particular, organic farms generate less carbon dioxide. Thus, buying organic products should reduce a family's carbon footprint. Organic produce, meats, dairy products, and eggs are becoming more widely available. Many prepared and processed foods, from canned beans to macaroni and cheese, are now made with organic ingredients.

But when many people go to the supermarket, they have a choice between buying local and buying organic. On one hand, this apple was raised without chemicals, but in a different state. On the other hand, that apple was raised using conventional farming techniques, but just a few miles away. It's not always obvious which apple has the smallest environmental impact. In some areas, the soil is very poor or the climate is not suited to growing particular sorts of crops. Growing things there often requires lots of extra chemicals, nutrients, and water. In these cases, food grown elsewhere may be more environmentally friendly. In other cases, the number of miles the products must travel before they are sold reduces the benefits of organic farming. Consumers need to do their own research based on where they live and what is available there to determine the best way to reduce their carbon footprint.

## Reduce, Reuse, Recycle

To reduce one's carbon footprint in the kitchen, one should think about the three Rs: reduce, reuse, and recycle. To reduce means to use less of something. To reuse means to use something again. To recycle means to prepare waste materials for reuse. In recent years, many people have focused on recycling. They think that they can buy anything as long as it or its packaging ends up in the recycling bin.

But actually, reducing and reusing are more important than recycling. Sorting recyclables, melting down cans and bottles, removing ink from paper, and other processes that prepare items to be remade into new things take energy. The amount of energy needed is often smaller than that required for harvesting raw materials to create new products. For this reason, recycling is important.

However, the process needs to start with reducing—using fewer goods that require energy to make in the first place. These things should then be used as many times as possible—reusing—before they go into

Many cities have programs that encourage residents to recycle paper, plastic, glass, cardboard, aluminum, and other materials. However, it's also important to reduce use overall and to reuse items as much as possible before recycling.

the recycling bin. This will make a bigger difference in the long run than simply consuming new products, using them once, and recycling them. The following chapters discuss ways to implement all three Rs in the grocery store, the kitchen, and eating beyond the kitchen.

# 2 At the Grocery Store

It's time to do the family grocery shopping. Buying certain products will help reduce a family's carbon footprint. Consumers should look carefully at the products they purchase. Questions to ask include the following: Is the product organic or conventional? How many food miles has it accumulated? How much energy was used to make this food? How much packaging does the product have?

To start, determine whether the product is organic or made of conventionally farmed ingredients. The U.S. Department of Agriculture (USDA) certifies that products are organic. Those that meet the standards display the USDA Organic seal. Other products may contain a mixture of organic and conventional ingredients. In general, organic products are produced using less energy than conventional products. But in some circumstances, a local conventional product is a better choice.

## Buying Local

Foods that travel a shorter distance travel fewer miles and thus require less energy for transportation. Most packaged foods provide an address for the company that produced them.

Some markets also label produce with the location where it was grown. Many stores stock baked goods from local bakeries, cheese and milk from local dairies, and so on. If a product came from a different state or country, however, it required lot of food miles, fuel, and energy to get to the store.

This USDA Certified Organic seal appears on the packaging for organic food. Foods must meet specific guidelines to be considered organic.

The food miles of a product may change depending on the time of year. When a fruit or vegetable is in season, it is probably being harvested in the area. For example, in April the supermarket may have strawberries from a local farm, but in November the strawberries are from Chile. Produce in season is often less expensive and more flavorful because it travels shorter distances. A local gardening or farmers' organization can provide information about when various kinds of local produce are available in your area.

It may be easier to find local products, especially produce, outside the traditional grocery store and supermarket. Farmers' markets, for example, are places where farmers sell fruits and vegetables directly to consumers. Some farmers' markets also offer dairy products, eggs, and meat from local producers. Since the sellers are the farmers themselves, they are very knowledgeable about how the food was raised. Prices are often lower than those in the supermarket because transportation costs

New York residents line up to select their weekly share of vegetables from a community supported agriculture (CSA) program. In some CSAs, boxes of produce are delivered to members' homes. CSA members pay for their shares of produce from a local farm in advance.

are reduced, packaging is eliminated, and the middleman—the supermarket—is cut out.

People who are unable to go to a farmers' market regularly may want to join a community supported agriculture (CSA) group. A CSA is a cooperative effort in which people pledge to support a local farm in return for a share of the farm's harvest. After paying a subscription fee, CSA members receive a box of fresh fruits and vegetables from the farm every week. The contents of the box change every time based on what is ready to harvest. Most CSAs provide recipes and instructions for preparation and storage with the produce. It's a great way to support local family farms, try new fruits and veggies, and increase the amount of fresh produce a family eats.

Buying less processed foods means more cooking. Vegetable soups like this one are a great way to use produce from a farmers' market, CSA, or supermarket.

## Buying Less

Any food that becomes stale in a cabinet or moldy in the fridge is a waste of the energy—not to mention money—it required to get from farm to home. At the grocery store, consumers should think carefully about how many people will be eating the food and how much they are likely to eat. Some families may find that they can help prevent wasted food by going to the grocery store more often and buying less each time. However, this must be balanced against the additional energy needed for driving to and from the supermarket.

Another way to reduce the amount of energy needed to produce the food a family consumes is to buy and eat less meat. It takes more energy to raise a pound of meat than a pound of grain. This is partly because animals eat grain, so farmers must raise the grain first and then feed it to the animals. If people eat the grain directly, it's more energy efficient.

Becoming a vegetarian, a person who eats no meat at all, is not necessary, but it would be a positive step. Eating just a few meatless meals a week will still make a difference. Some foods that many kids really like, such as macaroni and cheese, bean burritos, and peanut butter and jelly sandwiches, don't contain any meat. Other foods, such as stir-fry, lasagna, and curry, can easily be made meatless. There are even delicious meat-free alternatives to hamburgers and hot dogs.

## Reducing Packaging

Consumers should also consider the amount of material used to package the foods they eat. Buying foods in large rather than single-serving containers reduces the amount of packaging used. Imagine filling a large box of breakfast cereal with small, single-serving boxes of the same cereal. All of the cardboard from the single-serving boxes that isn't touching the cardboard of the large box is extra packaging for the same amount of food. This may seem like a small difference. But with millions of boxes of cereal sold every day, all that extra cardboard adds up. To reduce one's carbon footprint, it makes sense to buy large containers of foods like cereal and divide them into smaller, reusable containers at home.

Some foods can be bought without any packaging at all. Many stores have bulk food sections with bins of cereal, flour, pasta, grains, dried fruit, sugar, and other items. Consumers transfer only the amount they want to buy to a bag or other container. This is weighed to determine the price. At home, people generally transfer bulk foods to glass jars, plastic bins, or other sturdy reusable containers. Buying bulk products in small quantities can help prevent foods from going stale and being wasted. Bulk foods also reduce the amount of packaging needed.

When buying packaged foods, try to buy only foods that have packaging that can be recycled in the local area. Most cities have brochures and/or Web sites that explain what can be recycled there. For example, plastics are divided into seven different types, and many cities recycle only two or three of them. Buying products in recyclable packaging will save energy and reduce the waste sent to landfills.

## Greener Grocery Bags

At the supermarket checkout, a bagger generally loads a family's groceries into paper or plastic bags. Energy went into producing both kinds of bags. Trees were cut down to make the paper bags, and the plastic ones are difficult to recycle. Many people are realizing that neither paper nor plastic bags are very good for the environment. In 2007, San Francisco became the first U.S. city to outlaw plastic grocery bags. In Ireland, consumers pay twenty-two cents for every plastic bag they use. Other countries and locations in the United States are also considering making consumers pay for each bag or banning them entirely.

The most environmentally friendly option is to use cloth grocery bags instead of paper or plastic. Many supermarkets sell canvas bags with their logo on them. Some stores offer a five- or ten-cent credit for each reusable bag a customer brings in. Cloth bags can be washed with the regular laundry and kept in the car or on a hook near the door so that they are available whenever you head out for grocery shopping.

Reusable shopping bags like this one offer an alternative to plastic and paper bags. They are sturdy and washable.

Families that can't use cloth bags should reuse paper or plastic bags as many times as possible. This means taking them back to the supermarket so that they can be loaded with groceries again. Keep them in the car or near the door. Plastic grocery bags can also be used to line wastebaskets, pick up dog waste, or for other household purposes.

Paper bags that are torn and unfit for groceries can be shredded and mixed with food scraps in compost or recycled with other paper. However, many city recycling programs do not accept plastic bags. On the other hand, some grocery stores have bins where people can recycle used plastic grocery bags. The bags usually do not have to come from that particular store.

Of course, grocery bags are not the only bags a family receives at a store. Most consumers use clear plastic bags provided by stores for produce and bulk items. These bags can also be reused, though they may need to be rinsed out first. Reusable, lightweight mesh or tulle bags are also an option for produce and bulk items.

Finally, not everything needs a bag. A bag is useful to keep a pound of cherries together. One cucumber, however, probably does not need a bag. Making careful choices about when and when not to bag can reduce the number of bags used overall.

Once a person is home from the market and the groceries are put away, it's time to start cooking. The next chapter will examine some ways to reduce a family's carbon footprint while at work in the kitchen.

# 3 While Cooking

A family can reduce its carbon footprint while cooking in lots of different ways. Many of these are small changes that, over time, can make a big difference. The first is simply cooking more frequently. Buying foods with less packaging and processing generally means that they need more preparation at home. Rather than microwaving TV dinners, it's time to pull out pots and pans and learn cooking techniques that have gone out of style.

The previous chapter talked about wasting food by buying too much. Cooking too much food is also a waste. A family should prepare only as much food as it will eat, both initially and as leftovers. Although composting food recycles it, it's still better—and more economical—to throw out as little as possible.

## Preserving Food

Buying produce only in season, as suggested in the previous chapter, can become frustrating if few or no fruits and vegetables can be grown in an area in the winter. Canning, freezing, pickling, or drying local produce during the summer can provide a supply of fruits and vegetables throughout the year.

Local produce can be bought in the summer and fall and frozen. This way, you can enjoy locally grown fruits and vegetables in the winter and spring without having to buy expensive imported or long-distance produce that has a large carbon footprint.

In the last hundred years, technology has allowed vast quantities of fresh and frozen produce to be shipped between countries at all times of year. Previous to this kind of globalization, people preserved foods after they were harvested through canning and drying because few, if any, fresh foods would be available during the winter. Jam, tomato sauce, canned vegetables, and dried fruit made from local products and stored in containers that can be reused each year are likely to have smaller environmental impacts than simply buying commercial or imported versions of such products at the supermarket. This is because the commercial and imported versions have many more food miles and often come in containers that are not easy to reuse, such as tin or aluminum cans.

Preserving food can be a time-consuming but fun process. Many books and Web sites provide information on how to preserve food. An older relative or friend may be able to provide hands-on lessons. Homemade pickles and jams make great gifts, too.

The food preservation methods that make the smallest carbon footprint are those that do not require refrigeration during storage, such as canning. But freezing foods can also be useful. An empty freezer is an inefficient freezer. Thus, keeping it full of food helps save energy. Freezing leftover food can also help a family prevent waste. A freezer that is not full can be filled with bottles of water or scrunched newspaper to improve its efficiency.

## Using Energy Wisely

Paying attention to the season also helps to reduce energy use. During the summer, when it's warm, people should avoid using cooking methods that produce a lot of heat. Extra heat means that the air-conditioning must work harder to cool a home. This increases a family's energy use.

On the other hand, cooking methods that produce heat can help heat a home in the winter. After baking cookies, for example, leave the oven door open so that the heat inside can flow out and warm the surrounding rooms. The house's heater then doesn't need to work as much to keep the house at a comfortable temperature.

Matching the size of a pot to the size of a burner can save energy and help food cook faster. Placing lids on pots also helps keep the heat in.

When cooking on the stove, the pot or pan should fit the burner. If the pot is too small, heat escapes around the sides and is lost. Put lids on pots to help keep the heat in and reduce cooking time. In addition, only boil as much water as necessary for foods like tea and pasta.

When possible, use smaller appliances that require less energy. For example, a toaster oven easily bakes a few potatoes; using the full-size oven for only two or three little potatoes is not necessary. Another useful way to save energy is to cook things that need similar techniques at the same time. A casserole and a cake can share the oven. A pot of boiling water can cook both pasta and a steamer basket full of vegetables. In addition, heat may not be needed for the full cooking time. For example, in many cases it's possible to turn off the oven for the last few minutes of baking. As long as the oven door is closed, it should stay hot.

Other appliances should be turned off promptly after cooking. Toaster ovens, microwaves, and other small appliances use a small amount of energy even when not in use. This is especially true if they display the time or other information. By plugging all of them into a power strip, they can easily be turned on when needed and off at other times.

Some appliances, like the refrigerator, use energy all the time. When a refrigerator is open, cold air escapes. The fridge must then use more energy to cool itself down again. A person who knows what he or she wants before opening the fridge lets less cold air out. Refrigerator coils should also be cleaned at least once a year to help keep the appliance running efficiently.

When the lightbulbs burn out in the kitchen, replace them with compact fluorescent bulbs. According to the Energy Star program, compact fluorescent bulbs use about 75 percent less energy and last about ten times as long as ordinary incandescent lightbulbs.

## During and After the Meal

Families can also reduce their carbon footprints while eating a meal. At the table, avoid using paper plates, cups, and napkins, as well as plastic silverware. Eating off reusable dishes and then washing them requires less energy than creating and disposing of paper or plastic dishes. Plastic silverware can also be washed and reused. Cloth napkins can be used for multiple meals before being laundered if they aren't really dirty. Unless a family is very large and messy, using cloth napkins probably won't add any extra loads of laundry. In good weather, cloth napkins and dish towels—not to mention the rest of your laundry—can dry on a clothesline after washing. Running the dryer requires energy, but the sun is free, and it is gentler on your fabrics.

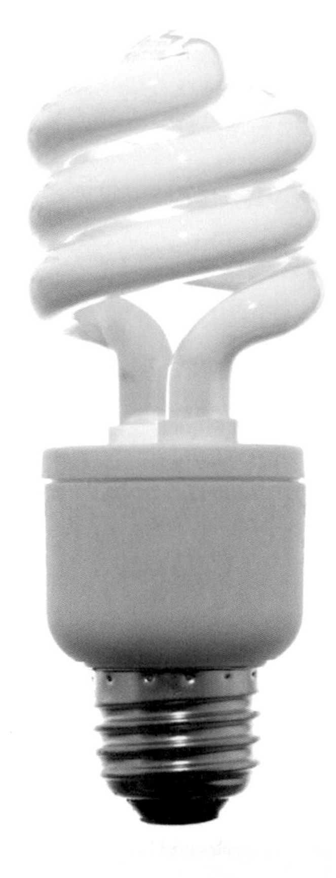

Compact fluorescent lightbulbs use less energy and last longer than incandescent light bulbs. They can be used all over the house, not just in the kitchen.

When cleaning up after a meal, use reusable sponges as well as cloth dishrags and dish towels. Avoid using paper towels if possible, and compost them when they are used. Dish soap and other cleaning products may be available in bulk or in recyclable packaging.

Keeping food containers sealed and the kitchen clean will help discourage pests from trying to dine there. Food eaten by insects is also a waste of energy and money. If a family does end up with pests in the kitchen, it should look into natural methods of eliminating them. The chemicals used in many insecticides are made out of fossil fuels, are often toxic to humans, and require energy to produce.

Run the dishwasher only when it is full. It uses the same amount of energy regardless of the size of the load. If time permits, turn off the dishwasher after the rinse cycle and let the dishes air-dry. This takes longer than the dry cycle on a dishwasher but uses less energy. When washing dishes by hand, fill a tub with hot soapy water for washing and another with warm water for rinsing, rather than letting the faucet run. Treating water to make it safe for human use, pumping it to a home, and then heating it all require energy. Saving water thus reduces a family's carbon footprint.

Before recycling the packaging from food products, determine if it can be reused first. Plastic containers from yogurt, cottage cheese, and other items can be washed and used to store leftovers in the refrigerator. Label them with a marker. Similarly, glass jars from pickles, spaghetti sauce, and other foods can be washed and used to store bulk foods. Other food packaging, such as coffee cans, cereal boxes, and egg cartons, may also be reusable as storage containers or materials for crafts and other projects. For example, a large coffee can decorated with colorful paper becomes a cookie jar. Seedlings for a backyard garden can be started in a paper egg carton. That same egg carton can also be used as a palette for finger paints or watercolors. Many books and Web sites discuss how to find new uses for food packaging. Be creative and environmentally friendly at the same time!

# 4 Beyond the Kitchen

Kitchens are the primary places where people use food. But food and food preparation are also important in other areas. Planting a garden, buying energy-efficient appliances and other kitchen equipment, and using reusable containers when eating and drinking away from home can also help reduce the carbon footprint a person has. The suggestions in this chapter will help families take their new awareness of global warming beyond the kitchen.

## Food in the Outdoors

One way to reduce "food miles" to "food feet" is by growing produce in a backyard garden. Picked just before cooking, these are the freshest veggies possible. People who live in apartments or houses without yards may be able to grow vegetables and herbs in pots on a balcony, patio, or windowsill. Many books, Web sites, and people in the local community can offer help with planting a garden.

Alternately, some cities have community gardens where local residents borrow or rent plots of land. These community gardens allow people without yards to grow their own food. Some schools are also starting their own gardens. These allow

Kids work in a community garden in New York. Community gardens provide people who do not have yards with land to grow vegetables and fruits. Many cities have community garden programs; some schools now have gardens for students as well.

students to learn about food production. They also provide vegetables and fruit for school cafeterias.

A backyard composter can turn food scraps into compost for a garden. Compost is full of nutrients that help plants to grow. It's also a great way to recycle many kinds of kitchen waste. Food-soiled paper and cardboard can be composted with food scraps. This includes paper towels, paper napkins, waxed paper, and parchment paper. Some community recycling programs will not accept any paper or cardboard that is food-soiled, so compost is a great way to recycle these items.

In addition, not all cooking takes place in the kitchen. In the summer, many families choose to cook outdoors on barbecue grills for at least some meals. Because the heat from barbecuing is released outside, a house's air-conditioning doesn't need to use as much energy to keep rooms cool. Barbecuing is more environmentally friendly if charcoal from local and sustainably managed forests is used. Families can also use solar energy to cook food in their backyard using a solar cooker. These devices trap or concentrate heat from the sun to warm food. Since solar cookers don't use fossil fuels, cooking in one doesn't contribute to a family's carbon footprint.

People who live in certain areas may also be able to forage for some foods. Fruits, berries, nuts, greens, and mushrooms are often available on public lands from city parks to national forests. Regulations vary, and a permit may be required. Thus, it's important to check with the park before starting to gather food. When foraging for the first time, go with someone experienced. Some kinds of mushrooms and berries are poisonous.

## Replacing Kitchen Equipment

Appliances, dishes, and other kitchen equipment should be used as long as possible in line with the first R: reduce. This includes repairing items when they stop working, rather than simply throwing them out and buying something new. Fixing an appliance can be a fun project and a good way to learn new skills. If the repair is beyond a family's skills, call a professional. If an item is not repairable, recycle it if possible.

If a family decides to replace still-functional utensils or other items, these can be donated to a thrift store or other charity. This way, others reuse the items, which extends their useful life before recycling. Although most people think about large housewares or department stores when they need to buy dishes or appliances, used versions of these items are often available at thrift stores and on Web sites. These are often at a lower cost or even free. Thrift stores and used bookstores can also be a good source of cookbooks. Most libraries have a cooking section, which allows people to try out cookbooks or copy recipes.

If purchasing new kitchen equipment, buy items that are of high quality and likely to last for a long time. Each spatula and spoon requires energy to create. If items wear out quickly, then more energy must be expended to produce new ones. Many new items are now made with recycled materials. This is often referred to as "post-consumer content." Buying such items supports recycling programs and helps them to continue. The kitchen equipment a family buys should also be recyclable when it is no longer functional.

When a family decides to buy a new appliance, it should choose an energy-efficient one. One way to do this is to look for the Energy Star label. Energy Star is a government program that awards the Energy Star label to household products that meet strict energy-efficiency standards, including dishwashers, refrigerators, and freezers. Using energy-efficient appliances reduces a family's carbon footprint and saves money on utility bills.

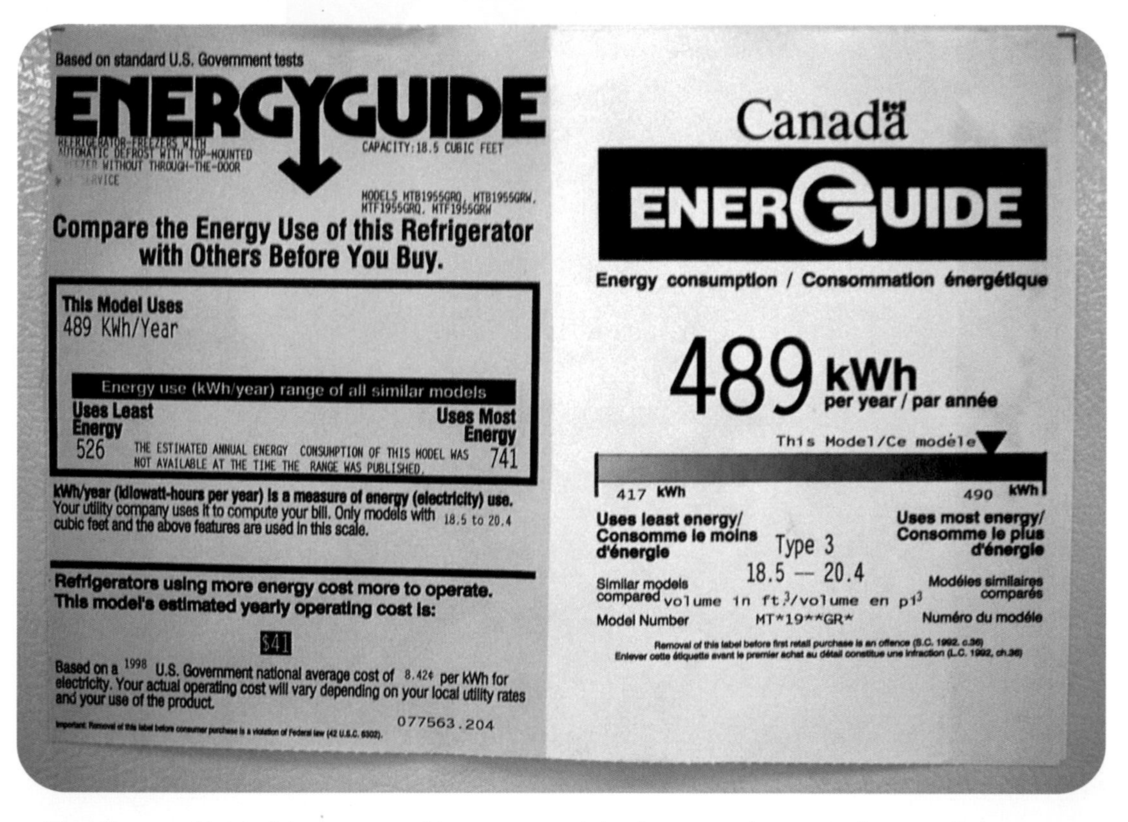

The Energy Guide label on a refrigerator explains how much energy it uses. Other appliances have similar labels. Choosing appliances that use the least amount of energy will help a family reduce its carbon footprint.

## Portable Food and Drink

Students eat in many places other than their homes: at school, at restaurants, in the car, at soccer practice, and so on. Many small changes can help make these meals more environmentally friendly.

Many students take lunch to school. Rather than using plastic or paper bags, try a reusable lunch box or bag. Sandwiches, salads, and other foods can be packed in reusable containers, rather than disposable

A wide variety of reusable bags, bottles, and other containers are available for school lunches, picnics, and other meals and snacks eaten outside the home.

plastic sandwich bags. If sandwich bags are used, they can be washed and reused to cut down on waste and energy use. In addition, reusable dishes and containers can be used to take food to potluck meals and picnics.

Reusable drink containers are also important. Many people drink bottled water, boxed juice, cans of soda, and other beverages in disposable single-serving containers. Single-serving portions require more packaging. Buy a reusable plastic or metal bottle and fill it with tap or filtered water. Many different companies sell pitchers or faucet attachments that filter water. Reusable bottles can also be used for juice, soda, and other beverages. Parents should use a reusable mug for their morning coffee.

When eating at a restaurant, diners can bring their own reusable containers to take home any leftover food. People can also encourage their favorite restaurants to provide environmentally friendly take-out containers. According to the *San Francisco Chronicle*, more than one hundred cities have banned restaurants from using take-out containers, cups, and other dishes made of polystyrene foam, often called Styrofoam. Restaurants in these cities use plastic or compostable paper containers instead.

Overall, people should determine which restaurants in an area serve organic food, compost, recycle, and in general do the same sorts of things that families are doing in their homes to make food and cooking more environmentally friendly. It's important to support these restaurants whenever possible.

## Get Active

It's important to make changes in one's own life. But the more people and organizations make environmentally friendly choices, the better off this planet will be. Thus, students should share their knowledge about carbon footprints with other people. This might be as simple as talking to other students. It could also mean writing an article for the school newspaper or encouraging organizations to do things differently. For example, students might encourage their schools to serve lunches on reusable dishes, to buy ingredients for cafeteria food from local farms, to start a garden, or to recycle food scraps.

Scientists are still debating just how much global warming may affect Earth and how quickly. But climate change is happening, and it's important for all people to do what they can to reduce their carbon footprints. The kitchen is a great place to start because everyone needs to eat every day. Some changes may seem small, but every little bit helps to reduce the amount of carbon dioxide released into the atmosphere. And lots of small changes can add up to some very big changes that will benefit all living things, humans included.

# Glossary

**agriculture** The raising of plants or animals, particularly those intended for use as food.

**carbon dioxide** The most common greenhouse gas and the one from which the term "carbon footprint" comes.

**carbon footprint** A measurement of the impact of human activities on the environment. This is generally calculated in units of carbon dioxide.

**climate change** The effects of global warming on the surface of Earth.

**community garden** A plot of land on which a group of people grows food.

**community supported agriculture (CSA)** A scheme in which people pledge to support a farm in return for a share of the farm's harvest.

**compost** A mixture of decaying organic matter, such as food scraps and dead leaves, that is used to fertilize gardens.

**consumer** A user or buyer of a product.

**conventional farming** Grown or made using traditional farming practices; usually used as the opposite of "organic farming."

**farmers' market** A market where farmers sell produce, meat, and other products directly to consumers.

**fertilizer** A substance that is used to add nutrients to soil.

**food miles** The distance a food travels from the farm to the consumer.

**forage** To look for food growing in natural areas.

**fossil fuel** Any material that is based on former life and can be burned, including oil, natural gas, and coal.

**global warming** An increase in the average temperature of Earth's atmosphere that causes changes in climate.

**green** The color associated with the environmental movement. People sometimes refer to becoming more Earth-friendly as "going green."

**greenhouse gas** Any of the gases that absorb sunlight in the atmosphere and thus contribute to global warming.

**organic** Describes something that is grown without chemical fertilizers or pesticides.

**packaging** The container in which a product is sold.

**produce** Fresh fruits and vegetables.

**recycle** To prepare waste materials for reuse.

**reduce** To lower the amount used of a certain material.

**reuse** To use again.

**sustainable** Able to continue with minimal effects on the environment.

**vegetarian** A person who does not eat any meat, fish, or poultry.

# For More Information

American Community Gardening Association
1777 Easy Broad Street
Columbus, OH 43203-2040
(877) 275-2242
Web site: http://www.communitygarden.org
This organization offers support and information to community gardeners and those who would like to start community gardens in the United States and Canada.

Canadian Organic Growers
National Office
323 Chapel Street
Ottawa, ON K1N 7Z2
Canada
(888) 375-7383
Web site: http://www.cog.ca
This organization supports farmers, gardeners, and consumers of organic products. It helps farms to transition from conventional to organic agriculture and educates the public about organic food.

Organic Consumers Association
6771 South Silver Hill Drive
Finland, MN 55603
(218) 226-4164
Web site: http://organicconsumers.org

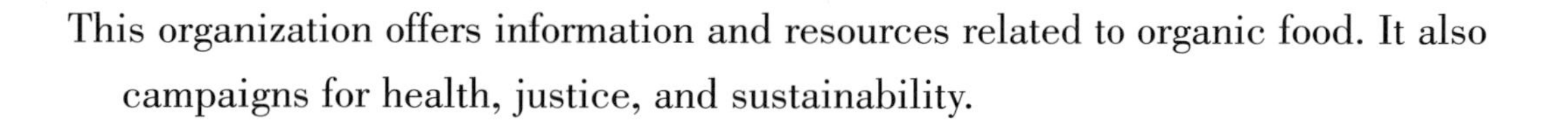

This organization offers information and resources related to organic food. It also campaigns for health, justice, and sustainability.

Post Carbon Institute
6971 Sebastopol Avenue
Sebastopol, CA 95472
(800) 590-7745
Web site: http://www.postcarbon.org

This organization provides research and education on issues related to the need to reduce energy consumption.

Slow Food USA
20 Jay Street, No. 313
Brooklyn, NY 11201
(718) 260-8000
Web site: http://www.slowfoodusa.org

This organization celebrates the slow food traditions in the United States (as opposed to fast-food culture and junk-food dietary habits). It emphasizes eating locally and sustainably. Slow Food Canada is online at http://www.slowfood.ca.

## Web Sites

Due to the changing nature of Internet links, Rosen Publishing has developed an online list of Web sites related to the subject of this book. This site is updated regularly. Please use this link to access the list:

http://www.rosenlinks.com/ycf/inki

# For Further Reading

Baines, John D. *Food for Life*. North Mankato, MN: Smart Apple Media, 2006.

Brezina, Corona. *Climate Change*. New York, NY: Rosen Publishing Group, 2007.

Dunn-Georgiou, Elisha. *Everything You Need to Know About Organic Foods*. New York, NY: Rosen Publishing Group, 2002.

Langholz, Jeffrey, and Kelly Turner. *You Can Prevent Global Warming (and Save Money!): 51 Easy Ways*. Kansas City, MO: Andrews McMeel Publishing, 2003.

Paladino, Catherine. *One Good Apple: Growing Our Food for the Sake of the Earth*. Boston, MA: Houghton Mifflin, 1999.

Sanger, Rick. *No Eat, Not Food: The Search for Intelligent Food on Planet Earth*. Grass Valley, CA: Mountain Path Press, 2006.

Spence, Christopher. *Global Warming: Personal Solutions for a Healthy Planet*. New York, NY: Palgrave MacMillan, 2005.

Thornhill, Jan. *This Is My Planet: The Kids' Guide to Global Warming*. Toronto, ON, Canada: Maple Tree Press, 2007.

Wilcox, Charlotte. *Recycling*. North Minneapolis, MN: Lerner Publications, 2007.

Winckler, Suzanne. *Planting the Seed: A Guide to Gardening*. North Minneapolis, MN: Lerner Publishing Group, 2002.

# Bibliography

American Community Gardening Association. "What Is a Community Garden?" Retrieved January 2008 (http://www.communitygarden.org/learn).

American Council for an Energy-Efficient Economy. "Consumer Guide to Home Energy Savings: Condensed Online Version. Cooking." August 2007. Retrieved January 2008 (http://www.aceee.org/consumerguide/cooking.htm).

Brower, Michael, and Warren Leon. *The Consumer's Guide to Effective Environmental Choices: Practical Advice from the Union of Concerned Scientists*. New York, NY: Three Rivers Press, 1999.

Carbon Footprint. "Reduce Your Carbon Footprint." Retrieved December 2007 (http://www.carbonfootprint.com/minimisecfp.html).

Gershon, David. *Low Carbon Diet*. Woodstock, NY: Empowerment Institute, 2006.

Goldsmith, Sheherazade. *A Slice of Organic Life*. New York, NY: DK Publishing, 2007.

Goodall, Chris. *How to Live a Low-Carbon Life*. London, England: Earthscan Publications, Ltd., 2007.

Goodyear, Charlie. "S.F. First City to Ban Plastic Shopping Bags." *San Francisco Chronicle*, March 28, 2007. Retrieved January 2008 (http://www.sfgate.com/cgi-bin/article.cgi?file=/c/a/2007/03/28/MNGDROT5QN1.DTL).

Government of Ireland. Waste Management (Environmental Levy) (Plastic Bag) (Amendment) (No. 2) Regulations 2007. Retrieved

January 2008 (http://www.environ.ie/en/Publications/Environment/Waste/PlasticBags/FileDownLoad,5063,en.pdf).

Horn, Greg. *Living Green: A Practical Guide to Simple Sustainability*. Topanga, CA: Freedom Press, 2006.

National Recycling Coalition. "Top 10 Reasons to Recycle." Retrieved January 2008 (http://www.nrc-recycle.org/top10reasonstorecycle.aspx).

Nelson, Laura, Jim Giles, Colin Macilwain, and Virginia Gewin. "Organic FAQs." *Nature*, 428, April 22, 2004, pp. 796–798.

ReusableBags.com. "Top Tips to Reduce Plastic (and Paper) Bag Consumption." 2007. Retrieved December 2007 (http://www.reusablebags.com/action.php?id=3).

Rogers, Elizabeth, and Thomas M. Kostigen. *The Green Book: The Everyday Guide to Saving the Planet One Simple Step at a Time*. New York, NY: Three Rivers Press, 2007.

Saunders, Caroline, Andrew Barber, and Greg Taylor. "Food Miles—Comparative Energy/Emissions Performance of New Zealand's Agriculture Industry." July 2006. Retrieved January 2008 (http://www.lincoln.ac.nz/story_images/2328_rr285_s9760.pdf).

Solar Cookers International. "How Solar Cookers Work." 2007. Retrieved January 2008 (http://solarcookers.org/basics/how.html).

Sonoma County Mycological Association. "Mushroom Picking Rules & Regulations." February 27, 2007. Retrieved January 2008 (http://www.somamushrooms.org/foraging/rules.html).

U.S. Department of Agriculture. "Community Supported Agriculture." January 22, 2008. Retrieved January 2008 (http://www.nal.usda.gov/afsic/pubs/csa/csa.shtml).

U.S. Department of Agriculture, Agriculture Marketing Service. "Farmers Market Facts: Who Benefits from Farmers Markets?" January 2007. Retrieved January 2008 (http://www.ams.usda.gov/farmersmarkets/farmersmarketbenefits.htm).

U.S. Department of Agriculture, Agriculture Marketing Service. "Organic Food Standards and Labels: The Facts." January 2007. Retrieved January 2008 (http://www.ams.usda.gov/nop/Consumers/brochure.html).

U.S. Department of Agriculture, Food and Nutrition Service. "Eat Smart—Farm Fresh! A Guide to Buying and Serving Locally-Grown Produce in School Meals." December 2005. Retrieved January 2008 (http://www.fns.usda.gov/cnd/Guidance/Farm-to-School-Guidance_12-19-2005.pdf).

U.S. Environmental Protection Agency. "Frequent Questions About Recycling and Waste Management." February 2008. Retrieved February 2008 (http://www.epa.gov/epaoswer/non-hw/muncpl/faq.htm).

U.S. Environmental Protection Agency and U.S. Department of Energy. "Energy Star: Appliances." Retrieved December 2007 (http://www.energystar.gov/index.cfm?c=appliances.pr_appliances).

U.S. Environmental Protection Agency and U.S. Department of Energy. "Energy Star: Light Bulbs and Fixtures." Retrieved December 2007 (http://www.energystar.gov/index.cfm?c=lighting.pr_lighting).

Zamora, Jim Herron. "Styrofoam Food Packaging Banned in Oakland." *San Francisco Chronicle*, June 28, 2006. Retrieved January 2008 (http://www.sfgate.com/cgi-bin/article.cgi?f=/c/a/2006/06/28/MNG65JLQJ411.DTL).

# Index

**A**

appliances, and reducing carbon footprint, 26–28, 30, 33–34

**B**

barbecuing, 33
bulk products, buying, 12–13, 20–21, 22, 23, 29, 30

**C**

carbon dioxide, 4, 5, 13, 37
carbon footprint, explained, 4–5
climate change, 4, 6, 9, 37
community gardens, 31
community supported agriculture (CSA) groups, 18–19
composting, 22, 24, 32–33, 37
cooking, and reducing carbon footprint, 24–30

**E**

eating outside home, 35–37
Energy Star program, 28, 34
energy use, reducing at home, 26–30, 31

**F**

farmers' markets, 17–18
farming, conventional vs. organic, 13–14, 16
food miles, 9–10, 14, 16, 17, 26, 31
food production, energy required for, 7–9
foraging, 33
forests, harvesting sustainably, 6
fossil fuels, 4, 5, 6, 8, 9, 10, 33

**G**

gardens
  community, 31
  growing your own, 31
  at school, 31–32, 37
global warming, 4, 31, 37
greenhouse gases, 4, 6
grilling, 33
grocery bags, 21–23
  reusing, 22–23
  using cloth, 21, 22
grocery store, reducing carbon footprint at, 16–23

**K**

kitchen equipment, repairing and replacing, 33–34

**L**

locally grown foods, 10–11, 13–14, 16–19, 24, 25, 37

**M**

meat, benefit of eating less, 19–20

**O**

organic foods, 14, 16, 37
  benefits of, 13

## P

packaging of food, 8, 9, 16, 18, 26, 29
energy required for, 11–12
reducing/reusing, 20–21, 24, 30, 36
preserving food, 24–26
processed foods, energy required for, 11

## R

recycling, 14–15, 21, 22, 24, 30, 32, 34, 37
"reduce, reuse, recycle," 14–15, 22, 30, 33, 34
reusable containers, 13, 20, 25, 30, 31, 35–36

## U

U.S. Department of Agriculture (USDA), 16

## V

vegetarian, becoming a, 20

## About the Author

Linley Erin Hall is a science writer and editor in the San Francisco Bay Area, California, one of the most environmentally aware and progressive areas of the United States. She has a B.S. degree in chemistry from Harvey Mudd College and a certificate in science communication from the University of California–Santa Cruz. She is a vegetarian who loves to cook and uses many of the suggestions in this volume in her own kitchen. This is her fifth book for Rosen Publishing. She is also the author of *Who's Afraid of Marie Curie? The Challenges Facing Women in Science and Technology*.

## Photo Credits

Cover (top left) © Jeff Greenberg/The Image Works; cover (bottom left) © www.istockphoto.com/Lucas Cornwell; cover (right) © Thinkstock/Corbis; pp. 5, 15, 24, 27, 31, 36 © Shutterstock; pp. 6, 10 © www.istockphoto.com/Tony Tremblay; p. 7 © Phil Schermeister/Corbis; p. 8 © Getty Images; p. 12 www.istockphoto.com/Lya Cattel; pp. 16, 22 © www.istockphoto.com/Yong Hian Lim; p. 18 © AP Photos; p. 19 © John Peacock; p. 25 © age fotostock/SuperStock; p. 29 © www.istockphoto.com/Mark Strozier; p. 32 © Rudi Von Briel/Photo Edit; p. 35 © Michael Newman/Photo Edit.

Designer: Les Kanturek; Photo Researcher: Marty Levick